101 Ways to Boost Your Writing Skills

by Linda Williams Aber

illustrated by Aija Janums

Troll Associates

ACKNOWLEDGMENTS

Special appreciation goes to a valued and respected teacher, Karen Irwin. Ms. Irwin appreciates the fact that all students learn differently, and recognizes that the "right" way to learn and the "right" way to write is the way that feels most comfortable to each individual. Thanks to Pushcart Press, Box 380, Wainscott, New York 11975 for permission to use quotations from *The Writer's Quotation Book,* edited by James Charlton.

For my mother, Phyllis W. Zeno,
the writer who encouraged me to be a writer too.

Contents

CHAPTER 1

All Write, All Ready!

Why does the word *write* make so many people feel wrong? As soon as the teacher asks the class to *write* something, kids in the front row freeze, kids in the middle row fidget, and kids in the back row roll their eyes upward in dread. If you're one of those kids in any of those rows, this book is for you. Keep it as handy as you would a television program guide. This will be your guide to writing the kinds of papers that will earn you the high marks you want.

The tried-and-true writing tips in this book are your ticket to freedom from the fear of writing. *Once you feel free, you'll discover that you can write, and you can write well.*

Does it surprise you to learn that being a good writer has nothing to do with being a good speller or a neatnik in penmanship? Writing has to do first with thinking, then organizing your thoughts, and finally putting the thoughts together in sentences. *The first steps are the same for everything you write: think, organize, write.*

Ideas, feelings, opinions, and observations are what make a writer different from just a speller. Some writers may have many thoughts and will write articles, essays, or books. Other writers will express their thoughts using fewer words. They may write poetry, songs, short stories, or plays. Still other writers may choose to communicate in even shorter formats. Bumper stickers, message T-shirts, and backs of cereal boxes were created by writers. *Remember, as soon as you write down even one of your thoughts, you are a writer.*

Writing is like any other activity. The more you do it, the better you get. Read through the suggestions in this book and try out some of the "This Is Not a Test" practice sessions. You'll see an improvement in your writing immediately. You'll sharpen your organization skills and your thinking skills. *If you can think, you can write, and with practice you can write better.*

Wisecracks and Wise Words from Famous Writers

Now that you know you are a writer, take a look at what some of your more famous fellow writers have said about their own writing experiences. You'll see that although writing can be serious, writers can be very funny.

Isaac B. Singer—"The wastebasket is the writer's best friend."

Peter De Vries—"I love being a writer. What I can't stand is the paperwork."

Dorothy Parker—"I can't write five words but that I change seven."

Robert Benchley—"It took me fifteen years to discover I had no talent for writing, but I couldn't give up because by that time I was too famous."

Somerset Maugham—"There are three rules for writing the novel. Unfortunately, no one knows what they are."

Steve Martin—"I think I did pretty well considering I started out with nothing but a bunch of blank paper."

Daphne du Maurier—"Writers should be read—but neither seen nor heard."

Lillian Hellman—"If I had to give young writers advice, I would say don't listen to writers talking about writing or themselves."

Here are some more serious words of wisdom from some other well-known writers.

Willa Cather—"Most of the basic material a writer works with is acquired before the age of fifteen."

Robertson Davies—"The most original thing a writer can do is write like himself. It is also his most difficult task."

Morely Callaghan—"There is only one trait that marks a writer. He is always watching. It's a kind of trick of the mind and he is born with it."

Katherine Anne Porter—"If I didn't know the ending of a story, I wouldn't begin. I always write my last line, my last paragraph, my last page first."

Lynne Reid Banks—"I think writing is very much like acting. As a writer you have to be in people's heads as if you are acting a role in a play. But if you are writing, you're acting the roles of several people, so you are head-hopping all the time."

E.B. White—"My own vocabulary is small, compared to most writers, and I tend to use the short words. So it's no problem for me to write for children. We have a lot in common."

William Faulkner—"Read, read, read. Read everything—trash, classics, good and bad, and see how they do it. Just like a carpenter who works as an apprentice and studies the master. Read! You'll absorb it. Then write. If it's good, you'll find out. If it's not, throw it out the window."

CHAPTER 2

The Write Stuff: What You Need to Write Right

1. Get comfortable. To write right, use the method of writing and the writing tools that suit you best.

If writing longhand allows you to feel more in control of your writing, choose a favorite pen or pencil and a notebook or pad of paper that opens flat.

If you write more slowly than you think, try dictating your thoughts into a tape recorder first. Then, listen to the tape and write down what you said.

If you don't like paper and pencil, learn to use a computer or a typewriter.

2. Before you get started writing, put together a set of reference books and keep them handy. A good reference library will have a dictionary, a thesaurus, an encyclopedia, and an English grammar book. Use the dictionary to check the meanings of words you are unsure of in your research. Use the thesaurus when you want to find a selection of

synonyms or words that are close in meaning to the word you want. An encyclopedia will put many subjects at your fingertips and will save you a lot of trips to the library. The grammar book will help you check your punctuation, sentence structure, and paragraph structure.

3. Find the right place for writing. Is it in your room? At the dining room table? At a desk in the family room? On a branch in your favorite tree? The right place is any place where you can have the tools, the time, the space, good lighting, and the level of silence you need to concentrate, to do creative daydreaming, and to write.

4. Choose a time of day or night that is right for writing. The right time is a time when you are alert and not distracted by a wish to be doing something else (like watching your favorite TV show). Let family members know you will be working and unavailable for phone calls.

5. Decide in advance exactly how long you will work, then stick to your schedule. Give yourself enough uninterrupted time to really get into your work. You decide what your time limit will be.

6. Once you are seated, stay there and work as long as you promised yourself you would. Some people find it helpful to set a kitchen timer for a designated length of time. Try it and see if it works for you. When the timer goes off, stop working or set it for an additional ten minutes so you can finish what you started.

7. Plan your work time well. Figure out how much time you will need to complete an assignment. First, of course, you must be sure how long your finished paper is supposed to be. If it is a long-term assignment, perhaps due in a week, divide your work time into equal amounts for each day. Don't save it all for the last night.

8. Reward yourself at the end of your writing time. You deserve it. A reward gives you something to look forward to after you've worked for a while. Here are some reward ideas.

- Have a huge hot fudge sundae.
- Take a bike ride around the neighborhood.
- Go in-line skating or roller skating.
- Take a ten-minute nap.
- Treat yourself to a bubble bath.
- Listen to your favorite music.
- Give yourself some uninterrupted telephone talk time.
- Sit and do absolutely nothing, without feeling lazy. After all, you've earned it!

CHAPTER 3

Start Write Now: How to Begin

9. "And your assignment is to . . . *write.*" Whether your assignment is to write a research paper, a personal narrative, a how-to paper, a persuasive paper, or descriptive paper, the steps to getting started are the same. Copy the following steps onto a sheet of paper and hang the paper above your desk or study area. Refer to this list before you begin your paper.
- Write down the assignment.
- Write down the date your assignment is due.
- Write down how long this assignment should be when it's finished.
- Write down specific format instructions, such as what the teacher wants included, (for example, name, date, subject of class, teacher's name, and so on),

10. Understand why you write. What is the purpose of your writing assignment? You need to know the answer to this question before you can start to write. There are four basic purposes for writing:

- To Express Yourself
- To Inform
- To Persuade
- To Be Creative

Are you writing simply to express your own feelings? Are you writing to give facts and other kinds of information? Are you writing to persuade other people to change their minds about something? Are you writing to create a story, a poem, or a play? Think about the assignment and ask yourself what your purpose is before you start to write. When you understand what your purpose is, you will be able to choose the right words, tone, and reference books.

To help figure out your purpose, look at the following four examples. All four examples have the same subject—a monkey escaped from the zoo. But each has a different purpose. As you read, think about how differently the subject is presented for each purpose.

Expressive Writing

I'll never forget the first time I saw Bomba at the Evanstown Zoo. It was a sunny Sunday afternoon, and the place was packed with people who were there to see the new monkey. I felt that Bomba was doing all of his tricks especially for me. If I waved at him, he waved at me. If I scratched my head, he scratched his head. A man standing next to me said, "Well, this monkey sure likes you!"

I thought the man was right, and I liked Bomba, too. I must have watched that little monkey for two or three hours straight. I never did get over to see the zookeepers giving the elephant a bath. Instead, I stayed by the monkey cage until I finally had to go home.

I felt sad to be leaving Bomba, and he seemed sorry to see me go. I promised him I'd be back again soon. Then I got busy with school work, soccer, and all kinds of other things. I was planning to go see Bomba again this weekend. Now an article in the newspaper says Bomba escaped yesterday. There's a big reward being offered for information leading to Bomba's return. I don't want any money. I just want Bomba to be back in his cage where he will be safe, and where I can keep my promise to come back and see him again.

Informative Writing

Monkey Escapes From Zoo

A monkey escaped from the Evanstown Zoo yesterday and zoo officials are offering a $1,000 reward for information leading to its safe return.

The spider monkey, known as Bomba, is brown and weighs ten pounds nine ounces. It was born in captivity and has always lived in a zoo.

Andrea Coleman, Associate Director of the Evanstown Zoo, advises the public against trying to capture the monkey if he is sighted. For the safety of the public and the monkey, special animal handlers will be available 24 hours a day. Anyone having any information about the missing monkey is asked to call Ms. Coleman at the special Missing Animals Hot Line number, 555-ZOOS.

Persuasive Writing

Dear Town Councilman Smith:

The escape of Bomba the monkey from the Evanstown Zoo is an important reminder of the need for a full-time guard at the zoo.

Due to cuts in the funding provided by the county, the hours of the zoo's guards have been cut in half. Instead of having two guards patrolling the fifteen-acre zoo grounds, there is now only one.

There are two obvious reasons to keep two guards on duty at all times. The first reason is for the safety and protection of the animals residing in the zoo. The second reason is for the safety and protection of the public. I urge you to vote "yes" on the bill before the council seeking to reinstate county funding for the zoo.

Sincerely,

Andrea Coleman

Andrea Coleman
Associate Director, Evanstown Zoo

Creative Writing

Run, Bomba, Run!

Run, Bomba, run! Little monkey's free.
Someone left the cage unlocked
Now where can Bomba be?
Run, Bomba, run! Little monkey, sees
People looking everywhere
Except up in the trees.
Run, Bomba, run! Little monkeys tease.
Bomba gladly will come back,
If they just say, "Please!"

11. Your writing speaks for you. Be sure to write as clearly as you speak. Use short words. Use familiar words. Learning to express your thoughts clearly allows others to know how much you know, what you're thinking, and what you want. Putting those thoughts down in a readable form allows others to "listen" to you even if you're not speaking to them face to face.

12. When it comes to big assignments, divide and conquer. Any job is easier when it is broken up into smaller jobs. Experienced writers follow some standard operating procedures. This helps them to get the job done, and it will help you too.

Imagine that your writing assignment is a big pie. There's no way you're going to be able to eat the whole thing in one sitting. You have a much better chance of finishing it if you divide it up and eat one piece at a time. Here's what your writing pie looks like. Divide every kind of writing assignment you have into these four easy pieces.

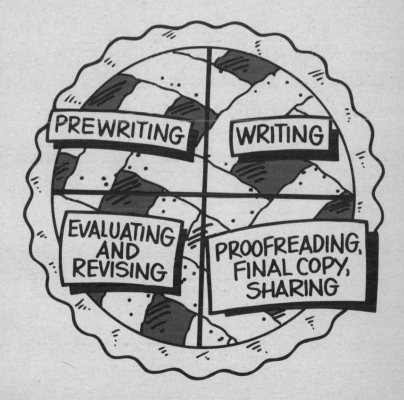

13. Here is a sample Writing Assignment Checklist to use as you go through the chapters in this book. This list will help you keep track of each step you should take to successfully complete a writing assignment.

Writing Assignment Checklist
✔✔✔

Assignment: _____

_____

Assignment Due Date: _____

Length of Finished Paper:

Minimum_____   Maximum_____

Prewriting Stage

The topic of this paper is:_____

My ideas of things to write about this topic are:

_____

_____

_____

I will present my ideas in this order:

_____

_____

_____

Writing Stage

First Sentence: _____

_____

Main ideas to be presented:

1. _____

_____

2. _____

_____

3. _____

_____

Concluding sentences: _____

_____

_____

Write title: _____

Evaluating and Revising Stage (Check as completed):

____Reread paper

____Correct spelling

____Correct grammar and punctuation

____Recopy for a perfect finished copy

____Turn in the paper

14. Writing assignments begin the same way for all writers. A blank piece of paper or a blank computer screen seems to stare, well, blankly back at you. It can feel scary to look at that empty space and realize it's your job to fill it. Greet your blank piece of paper as you would a friend. In fact, like a good friend, it will accept anything you want to say. It is your place where you can speak out of turn, make mistakes, have strong opinions, reveal your secrets, and display your knowledge. And, because it is your paper, you can change your mind and start over as often as you wish.

15. Write about things you are really interested in. Your teacher will give you a general subject to write about. Maybe you'll like the subject, or maybe you'll think it's totally boring. You can make the subject easier to write about by making it more personal. If the subject is very general, narrow it down to something more specific. For example, if the general subject is The Ancient Egyptians, you might choose to write about the first time you saw the mummies at a museum. Then read to find out information about why people were mummified and how the mummies were preserved. Write about your findings.

CHAPTER 4

Prewriting: Get the Write Ideas

16. Think before you write. As soon as you hear the assignment, start working on it in your head. Think about the subject or topic, and make a mental note of anything that comes to your mind related to that topic. Ask yourself questions about the topic. What is interesting about it? Who would be interested in it? Why is it important to understand the topic? How can you make it interesting to yourself? Answering these questions will help you figure out what slant or angle you might bring to the subject.

17. If you are asked to write about a personal experience such as your summer vacation, narrow the topic down. Think about the summer vacation. Try to remember one day that was special. Try to remember one hour in that day that was very special. Try to remember one specific thing that happened in that hour that was very, very special. Write about it.

18. Choose a topic you won't mind sharing with your readers. If you are going to write about something personal, be sure it is something you want your teacher and the other students in your class to know.

19. Try the free-thinking strengthening exercise on page 33 just for fun. It will help you see how to take a topic and think about it creatively. No writing allowed. Think!

This-Is-Not-A-Test Exercise # 1:
Think!

The subject or topic is Fast Food Restaurants.

A. Think of three reasons why these eating places are called "fast food restaurants."

B. There's a new fast food place coming to your town. It serves only healthy food. Think of a name for the place.

C. You are working for a local newspaper. It is your job to write an article about the new fast food place in town. Think of three things you want your readers to know about the place.

D. Think of one funny thing that might happen the first day the fast food restaurant is open to the public.

E. Think of one customer in the restaurant and describe him or her to yourself in detail. Think of three things that might be in this customer's wallet.

F. Think of one thing this customer might think about on the way home from the new fast food restaurant.

20. Use your imagination, but also keep your ears and eyes open. Although you may sometimes feel that your mind is a total blank, you can fill in that blank by noticing and recognizing the ideas that are all around you.

21. Start a journal. Don't worry about neatness, grammar, or punctuation. This journal is your sourcebook for ideas. Use a blank book, a spiral notebook, or even a file folder with loose sheets of paper. Write down your observations, feelings, experiences, opinions, great ideas, and questions you have. Keep your journal handy so you can write whenever you feel inspired.

22. Use your journal to collect favorite poems, quotations, words from songs, newspaper cartoons that make you laugh, jokes, or anything else you like.

23. Write down your dreams and daydreams. Make up story ideas or poems based on those dreams, or write down what you think your dreams may mean. Try to write the best dream you could have. Or write a dream that would scare you if you had it.

24. Make a word bank in your journal. Start keeping a list of new words you learn, words you like the sound of, words that describe feelings you have, words you hear in songs, words you overhear in other people's conversations. Keeping a word bank keeps you on the lookout for more and more words to add to your bank. Collecting words can be as much fun as collecting stickers, or cards, or anything else.

25. Write every day at a certain time. Make your journal a habit.

26. Write the date on each journal entry so you'll remember later when these ideas were important to you.

27. Look through your journal every once in a while just to remind yourself of the ideas you've collected. If you have included something you like, think about why you like it. Does it bring back a special memory? Does the idea mean as much to you now as when you first wrote it down? Why do you think your feelings may have changed?

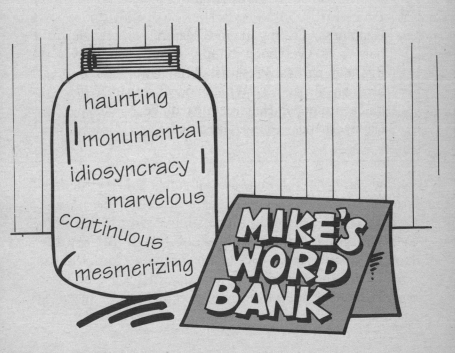

28. Try free writing with nothing specific in mind. Set a timer for three minutes. Then write whatever comes into your mind at the moment. Don't worry about full sentences or even sensible sentences. Feel free to free write!

29. Try free writing with a specific word in mind. Look at this example of free writing based on the word *happiness*.

Happiness

Happiness. Feeling happy. Making others feel happy. Is everybody happy? Happy birthday. Birthday parties. Presents. What I want for my birthday. A new CD. What kind of music? What kinds of songs? Happy songs make me happy. Happy Birthday to me. Happiness.

Now you try it. Fill in a word of your choice in the free-writing exercise on page 33. Set a timer for one minute, then write what comes into your mind. Why do you think these images came to mind about this word? Try this exercise again in a few days using the same word. Did you write down the same thoughts? Try this exercise with a friend. Did he or she write down thoughts similar to yours?

This-Is-Not-A-Test Exercise # 2:
Free Writing

_____

_____

_____

_____

_____

_____

_____

_____

_____

30. Make a list of things you think about all the time. It might be baseball, friends, food, horses, boys, girls, video games, or anything else. Your list will provide you with ideas to write about. It will also show you what your interests are so you can relate those interests to almost any topic. For example, if you are assigned the topic "Great Inventions," you might realize from seeing "baseball" on your list that you would be interested in finding out about the invention of the pitching machine. Use your list to help you find your personal relationship to the general topic assigned.

31. Details are every little thing, and they are a very big thing in good writing. Touch, sound, smell, taste, and sight provide all the sensory details needed to make your writing come alive. Sometimes your teacher might ask you to "write more." Let's say the topic is "Walking to School." You could write:

Walking to School

I left my house and turned right at the end of my driveway. On my way to school I saw other houses that looked just like mine. There were kids waiting on the corner for the bus to come. Because I was late, I had to hurry, so I didn't see too much besides that.

You may feel you've said all there is to say about what you saw on the way to school that morning. How can you stretch it out to fill the one page that is required? Add details. Here is a sample list of sensory details you could have collected on your walk to school:

Touch: front door handle felt cold; air was icy and crisp; hood of my jacket felt scratchy on the back of my neck; ground felt hard and frozen.

Sound: dog barking; car engine running; crunching of ice under feet; kids laughing at bus stop.

Smell: bacon cooking next door; exhaust from idling car; air smells crisp and clean.

Taste: bagel and cream cheese, orange juice, toothpaste.

Sight: frosty smoke from breath in cold air; grass white with frost; snow clouds hanging overhead; dog scratching at door to get in; kids huddling together to keep warm at the bus stop; neighbor scraping ice off car window; Mom standing at the window waving; houses along the street— one with red door, one with blue door, one with white door, two with black shutters.

Once you have gathered these details, you will use words to paint the picture of what you saw. Don't just *tell* them what you saw. *Show* them. Here is an example of a sentence that *tells* and one that *shows:*

Tell: It was cold outside.

Show: Ice crunched beneath my feet, and my breath filled the air with crystal clouds.

With all of these details gathered from your five senses, it should be much easier for you to write more about "Walking to School." Try writing a first paragraph in the just-for-fun exercise on page 40. Use as many details as possible in each sentence. And remember, don't tell your readers. Show them.

This-Is-Not-A-Test Exercise # 3:
Using Your Senses

Title: Walking to School

Opening sentence: _____

_____

_____

Detail sentence: _____

_____

_____

Detail sentence: _____

_____

_____

Detail sentence: _____

_____

_____

32. You can collect some good descriptive details by asking yourself these questions about your subject:
- What is most noticeable about my subject?
- What are the most important features of my subject?
- What smells, sights, sounds, tastes, and feelings will help my reader imagine my subject in more detail?
- What factual details are important?
- What details can I collect from reading about my subject?
- What details can I make up?

33. When you are assigned a topic which you cannot write about from personal experience or observation, read books, magazine articles, and newspapers for specific information. As you read about your topic, look for the main ideas. Then try to find details in your references to support those ideas.

34. When you read for information, don't read everything. Skim through the table of contents, the index, and chapter titles and subtitles. You will be able to pick up some good general information without spending a lot of time poring over one book.

35. As you come across information that is valuable for your topic, read slowly and carefully. Take notes on the main ideas and the details supporting them. Many students find it helpful to organize their notes on index cards. You can use one or two index cards per book. Make sure your handwriting is neat so you can read and organize your notes later on.

36. When you look over your notes, cross out the details you know you won't need. Number the remaining details in the order you might want to use them. If you change your mind later, simply renumber your notes.

37. As you read about your topic, look for the answers to these six questions: Who, When, Where, Why, What, and How. For example, let's say your topic is "Travels of Marco Polo." Skim encyclopedias and history books for brief answers to these questions. After you've gathered this basic information, your first notes might look like this:

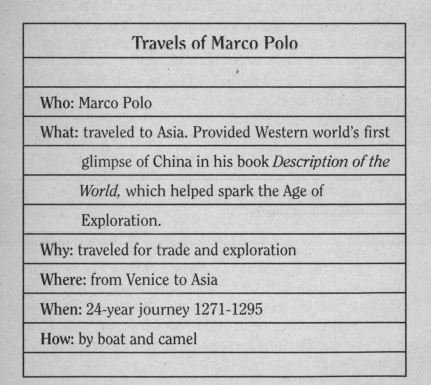

Travels of Marco Polo
Who: Marco Polo
What: traveled to Asia. Provided Western world's first
glimpse of China in his book *Description of the*
World, which helped spark the Age of
Exploration.
Why: traveled for trade and exploration
Where: from Venice to Asia
When: 24-year journey 1271-1295
How: by boat and camel

These simple answers to the five questions provide you with a beginning outline for your paper. Your next step will be to read information and fill in the details.

38. Know when to say "when!" At some point in your information gathering and idea collecting you have to stop and move on to the writing. If you have followed the suggestions in this chapter, you are ready to stop prewriting and start writing. Congratulations!

CHAPTER 5

Great Beginnings:
Opening Sentences

39. When you have gathered all the information you need, organize it before you start writing. You don't have to write in complete sentences. Just make notes to refer to as you start to write your paper. Use the Writing Assignment Checklist in Chapter 3 to help you put your ideas and facts in order of importance.

40. Look over your list of ideas and facts to see how they relate to each other. Group them together in a logical order. One way to do this is to make a chart similar to the one on page 46. Use the chart to fill in the facts and ideas that relate to each question.

✐ Get-the-Facts-In-Order Chart

Facts Relating to Who:_____

_____

_____

Facts Relating to What: _____

_____

_____

Facts Relating to Why: _____

_____

_____

Facts Relating to Where: _____

_____

_____

Facts Relating to When:_____

_____

_____

Facts Relating to How:_____

_____

_____

41. Before you begin to write your first sentence, remember: A sentence is a group of words that tells a complete thought. A complete sentence has a *subject,* which tells whom or what the sentence is about, and a *predicate,* which tells what the subject does or is. Without both parts, the sentence is a *fragment,* or only a part of a complete thought.

42. Remember what you already know. There are four kinds of sentences: questions, statements, commands, and exclamations. Your writing will be more interesting if you use all four kinds of sentences when you write instead of just one or two. Here are examples of each kind of sentence:

• A question asks something and ends with a question mark: Where is Bomba?

• A statement tells something and ends with a period: Bomba is a small spider monkey.

• A command tells you to do something and usually ends with a period. If the command is one showing strong feeling, it ends with an exclamation point: Go to the zoo. Watch out for that lion!

• An exclamation is a statement showing a strong feeling and ends with an exclamation point: I found the lost monkey!

43. When you begin writing a paper remember this well-known advice to writers: *"Tell them what you're going to say. Say it. Then tell them what you've said."* Your opening sentence should, *"Tell them what you're going to say."*

44. An opening sentence or even first paragraph is called your "lead." Plan your first sentence so that it leads your reader in the right direction for the rest of the paper. Your lead sentence will give the reader your main idea. All the sentences that follow your lead will be details that support the main idea.

45. A good opening sentence should make your reader curious enough to want to find out more. For example:

Opening Sentence:
The mud oozing down the side of the mountain crept slowly toward the small cabin in the valley below.

or

Opening Sentence:
No one in the town of Bedford wanted to admit that they believed in U.F.O.s.

46. Write a first sentence that makes your reader care about what you are going to say. You can do this by teasing the reader with information that affects them. For example, a paper about water pollution might start out like this:

Opening Sentence:
 Are you poisoning yourself every time you take a sip of water from your home faucet?

Or, add a familiar human being to your paper, someone your readers would be likely to recognize as a general type of person they might know. It will "humanize" your topic. For example:

Opening Sentence:
 When my grandmother turned on the faucet in the bathroom, we heard her screams all the way downstairs.

47. Don't be too specific. While it's important to make sure your subject is not too broad, it's just as important to make sure your subject is not too specific. For example, if the general topic is whales, you should not write about all whales. Choose a specific kind of whale, but don't write just about the babies. Let your reader know all about the whale you chose—what it looks like, what it eats, how big it is, how long it lives, and so on.

48. Take the time to try out a few different opening sentences. Read over each attempt and ask yourself, "Does this sentence tell the reader what I'm going to say? Does it make the reader curious to know more?"

49. Decide what main idea you want to get across. For example, your main idea for a paper about the blue whale might be that biologists find them fascinating because they are the largest animals ever to be on Earth. Not only is that the main idea, it's also a fascinating piece of information.

50. Your opening sentence should do three things:
 • Catch your reader's attention.
 • Introduce your subject.
 • Set the mood for the rest of the paper.

Here are two possible opening sentences for a paper on the blue whale.

Opening Sentence:

Blue whales are fascinating to scientists because they are the largest animal ever to have lived on Earth.

    or

Opening Sentence:

Blue whales just might be the heavyweight champions of the animal world.

51. If you are writing a paper in which you want to show both feelings and facts, don't be afraid to add some emotion to an opening sentence. Let's say you are writing about your favorite teacher leaving your school. Give the reader the facts and show how you feel about it. Here are examples of sentences that draw the reader in using feelings as "bait."

Opening Sentence:

Mrs. Purnell's announcement that she was leaving our school was as surprising as the tears I suddenly felt welling up in my eyes.

or

Opening Sentence:

I never knew a teacher could mean so much to me until the day I found out Mrs. Purnell was leaving.

or

Opening Sentence:

The sound of muffled crying filled the auditorium as the principal stood on the stage and read the announcement that Mrs. Purnell was leaving.

52. Begin at the beginning. Don't waste words working up to the beginning. The following sentence is a genuine word-waster!

Opening Sentence:

I would like to write about Maniac Magee so that you will find out why he is such a cool kid.

Here's a better beginning that gets right to the subject.

Opening Sentence:

Maniac Magee can outrun, outthrow, and outsmart anyone.

53. The opening sentence is the beginning of your opening paragraph. A paragraph is a group of sentences that work together to help the reader understand the main idea. Each sentence in your opening paragraph should add a detail related to the main idea in your opening sentence. For example:

Opening Paragraph

Opening sentence: Blue whales just might be the heavyweight champions of the animal world.
Supporting sentence: They grow to be one hundred feet long and weigh one hundred and fifty tons!
Supporting sentence: In fact, scientific studies show the blue whale is the largest animal that has ever lived on Earth.

Opening Paragraph

Opening sentence: I never knew a teacher could mean so much to me until I found out that Mrs. Purnell was leaving.
Supporting sentence: She was more than just a great English teacher.
Supporting sentence: Mrs. Purnell was my friend.

Opening Paragraph

Opening sentence: Maniac Magee can outrun, outthrow, and outsmart anyone.
Supporting sentence: In Jerry Spinelli's book, *Maniac Magee,* a 12-year-old orphan boy named Maniac Magee amazes everyone when he seems to appear out of nowhere to be the hero in every situation.
Supporting sentence: He uses his incredible athletic abilities to win races, but perhaps his greatest talent is winning the respect and admiration of everyone he meets.

54. If you have followed the suggestions in this chapter, you have learned how to write an effective opening sentence and first paragraph. Now you are ready to develop your main idea and fill in the middle of your paper. Congratulations!

CHAPTER 6

Great Middles: Paragraphs with Punch

55. Remember the advice, "Tell them what you're going to say. Say it. Then tell them what you've said." The middle of your paper is the part where you "Say it."

56. Don't let the idea of a paragraph scare you. Remember, a paragraph is only a group of sentences that tell about one main idea. You already know how to write sentences. Now it's just a matter of putting those sentences together in an order that is logical and sensible.

57. The first sentence in a paragraph is indented. Every time you begin a new paragraph, be sure to indent a few spaces to the right of the margin of your paper. Remember to indent the same number of spaces each time you begin a new paragraph.

58. Write a topic sentence for each paragraph you will write in your paper. Ask yourself, "What do I want to say in this paragraph?" Say it and then support it with details as you learned to do in Chapter 5.

59. Vary the length of your sentences. Too many short sentences or too many long sentences in a row can get monotonous.

60. Keep your paragraphs short. It's better to have more paragraphs with fewer sentences than fewer paragraphs with more sentences. Short paragraphs make a paper faster to write and clearer to read.

61. Learn to move smoothly from one paragraph to the next. The word or group of words that moves the reader from one paragraph to the next is called the *transitional* word or phrase. This word or phrase shows your reader that there is a connection between what he or she has just read and what is coming in the next paragraph. Here are some examples of words that show connections in time and place.

Transitions showing time: after, at last, before, eventually, finally, first, meanwhile, next, then, when

Transitions showing place: above, across, around, before, behind, beyond, down, in, inside, next, over, there, under

62. A good paragraph is one in which each supporting sentence fits together with the other sentences. Make sure each sentence you write in the paragraph really belongs in that particular paragraph. For example, if you are writing about apple-picking, don't confuse your reader by listing the equipment needed and then throwing in a sentence about how much you like to eat apple pie. Organize your apple-picking paper's paragraphs like this:

Paragraph 1: Who goes apples picking? When is the best time to go?

Paragraph 2: What equipment is needed for apple picking?

Paragraph 3: Where is the apple orchard? What does your favorite orchard look like?

Paragraph 4: What kinds of apples do you pick? Why do you like picking your own apples instead of buying them?

Paragraph 5: What you do with the apples after you've picked them?

63. Even if you are creating a story, your paragraphs need to be in a logical order. For example, let's say your story is about two kids taking a day off from school and going to an amusement park instead. Your writing job is easier if you present the story's events in paragraphs that naturally follow each other. You might organize your creative story about "The Day the Ferris Wheel Got Stuck" like this:

Paragraph 1: Introduce the characters and let the reader know they are headed for trouble. They are playing hooky from school and will go to the amusement park.

Paragraph 2: Tell where they meet and how they get to the park.

Paragraph 3: Describe what the amusement park looks/ sounds/smells like when they arrive.

Paragraph 4: How do the characters feel when they get there? Happy? Nervous? Free? Scared?

Paragraph 5: What do the characters do when they get to the amusement park? Why is the Ferris wheel their favorite ride?

Paragraph 6: Describe the terrible thing that happens. After spending the whole day there having a great time, the characters decide to make their last ride the Ferris wheel. The Ferris wheel gets stuck, the photographers and news reporters come, and the characters know now they will be on the evening news—caught playing hooky!

Paragraph 7: Describe how the characters respond to what happens. What conclusion do they come to and what have they learned?

64. When you are writing a short, factual report, think of it as a pyramid. Imagine that your readers only have a minute. They want to find out as much as possible before they have to go. Keeping that fact in mind, make sure your first paragraph answers all the who, what, where, when, why, and how questions. With each additional paragraph, add more information and more details.

Paragraph Pyramid

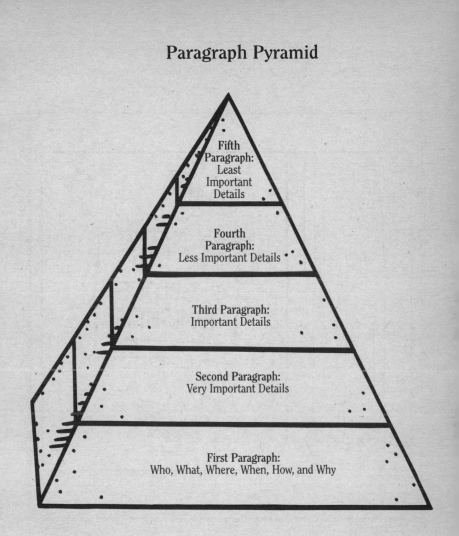

65. When you have written your opening sentence, opening paragraph, and detailed supporting paragraphs, you are ready to start working on the ending. Your paper is almost finished. Congratulations!

CHAPTER 7

The End Is Near: Fabulous Finishes to Fantastic Papers

66. How do you know when you've really reached the end?

- When the problem has been solved
- When the instructions are complete
- When the opinion has been expressed
- When the information has been given

You are now ready to write your closing paragraph. Read over your notes and compare them with your paper. What do you think? Have you said everything you want to say? Yes? Great! Then you are almost done. Now comes the time to write your ending. This is where you think back to the well-known advice to writers, and **"Tell them what you've said."**

67. When it comes to writing your ending, here's the best writing "trick" in the book: End your paper by bringing it back to the beginning. Write a closing sentence that reminds your reader of your opening sentence. For example:

Opening Sentence:
When my grandmother turned on the faucet in the bathroom, we heard her screams all the way downstairs.

Closing Sentence:
Thanks to Grandmother's screams when she saw brown water coming out of the faucet, the problem was solved and our running water is no longer water from which we are running!

68. Restate your main idea. Your last paragraph should have a clear conclusion so your reader isn't left hanging. Use the last paragraph to restate your main idea, using different words. Here's an example:

Opening Sentence:
Blue whales are fascinating to scientists because they are the largest animal ever to have lived on Earth.

Restate Main Idea in Closing Paragraph:
The behavior of all whales is interesting to scientists, but it is definitely the blue whale that captures the most attention. As long as it is the heavyweight champion of the animal world, scientists will be watching with an interest as great as the blue whale itself.

69. End with a summary. Read your rough draft again and use a marker to highlight the major points you've made. Summarize those highlighted points in your final paragraph. For example:

Opening Sentence:
Are you poisoning yourself every time you take a sip of water from your home faucet?

Summary Closing Paragraph:
Water is indeed one of our most precious commodities. The public water filtration system cannot be a thing local governments ignore until brown water starts pouring out of all the citizens' faucets. It must be monitored, maintained, and modernized as needed. In this country, where money flows as freely as water, let some of that money be put toward keeping the water flowing freely and free of contamination.

70. Give one last example. Don't introduce any new ideas or new material in your final paragraph. However, you can close your paper with one more example of the main idea.

Opening Sentence:
I never knew a teacher could mean so much to me until the day I found out Mrs. Purnell was leaving.

Last Example Closing Paragraph:
With tears in my eyes, I said good-bye and hugged Mrs. Purnell. That last hug reminded me of all the hugs she had given to me throughout the school year. I realized then that all those hugs, plus this last one, would add up to a wonderful memory of Mrs. Purnell, the best teacher in the world.

71. Offer a final comment in the form of a personal observation about your subject, or even a prediction about what might happen in the future regarding your subject.

Opening Sentence:
Maniac Magee can outrun, outthrow, and outsmart anyone.

Final Comment Closing Paragraph:
Everywhere Maniac went he left someone feeling better than before he came. It's great to be able to run fast and throw a ball far. It's even greater to be able to think fast and use that talent to survive. However, Maniac's great sensitivity to the feelings of others was the quality that would win him a prize in the biggest race of all, the human race.

72. End with a request of your readers to take action. Conclude with a paragraph urging readers to use what they've learned in your paper to change their own thinking or persuade others to change.

Opening Sentence:
The escape of Bomba the monkey from the Evanstown Zoo is an important reminder of the need for a full-time guard at the zoo.

Request for Action Closing Paragraph:
Keeping in mind the safety and protection of the animals residing in the zoo, the decision about reinstating county funding should be an easy one to make. Left unguarded, the animals are at risk of finding their own way out of the cages, or having an unfriendly visitor finding his way into the cages. A "yes" vote on the Zoo Funding Bill before the

council is a vote to protect the animals in the Evanstown Zoo from harm.

73. Continuity of feeling is important. Your closing sentence should relay the same mood or feeling as your first sentence. If you began your paper with a humorous sentence, end it with a humorous sentence that reminds the reader of the first one. If you began seriously, end seriously.

74. If you have written your closing paragraph and your last sentence, you only have one more thing to write: *The Title*. Although it is the first thing to appear on your paper, some people like to wait until the entire rough draft is written before deciding what title is appropriate. Your title should give the reader some idea of your subject, details, main idea, and the tone of your paper.

75. A title has a very important job to do. It must catch your reader's attention and interest. How can you do that with just a few words? There are several ways.

- Make your reader laugh—*King Kong Move Over, Bomba's Coming!*
- Make your reader curious—*How the Monkey Got Away*
- Make your reader feel involved—*Only You Can Save the Zoo*
- Ask your reader a question—*Where's Bomba Now?*
- Tell your reader the subject—*The Day the Monkey Ran Away*

---

76. If you have written a straightforward, factual paper, write a title that sums up the subject. For example:

Main Topic: Water pollution in my town
Title: *A Town without Water*
Title: *Caution: This Water Not Suitable for Drinking*
Title: *The Water Is Running . . . Out*

---

77. If you have written a personal narrative filled with feeling and emotion, write a title that tells the reader that. For example:

Main Topic: My teacher is leaving
Title: *Good-bye Mrs. Purnell*
Title: *Best Wishes to the Best Teacher*
Title: *A Teacher to Remember*

---

78. A title should tell your subject clearly and immediately. If you choose to write a funny title, add a colon and then a more serious title following it. For example:

- *Monkey See, Monkey Doesn't See: A Little Monkey's Big Escape*
- *A Whale of a Tale: The Facts About Blue Whales*

---

79. Write your title, and then give it the Title Test. Ask these questions:

- Does this title make a good first impression on the reader?
- Does this title tell the reader what this paper is about?
- Does this title catch my reader's attention and interest?

If the answers are yes, then you have finished your rough draft. Now you are ready to go on to the next step: Evaluating, revising, correcting, and all-around cleanup. Pat yourself on the back, stand up and stretch, and accept the congratulations you deserve!

CHAPTER 8

All-Purpose Evaluation and Revision Kit: Fix It Up, Copy It Over, and Turn It In

80. The draft is done and it's good. Now it's time to make it very good, even great! Reading over your paper to find where it needs improvement in content, organization, language, or style is called evaluation. When you do the evaluating you have the opportunity to find mistakes *before* your teacher finds them! More importantly, you've worked hard on this paper. Make it the best work you've ever done. Use the Evaluation Checklist on page 70 when you read over your paper.

Evaluation Checklist
✔✔✔

Yes____ No____ Does my title catch my reader's attention?

Yes____ No____ Does my introduction draw my reader into the paper?

Yes____ No____ Is the opening paragraph easy to understand?

Yes____ No____ Is every group of words a complete sentence?

Yes____ No____ Do all the sentences in each paragraph support the main idea?

Yes____ No____ Should I take out any sentences?

Yes ____ No____ Is each paragraph clearly linked to the paragraph before and after it?

Yes____ No____ Does my conclusion restate my main idea?

Yes____ No____ Does my conclusion leave my reader with a sense of completeness?

Yes____ No____ Does my last sentence remind my reader of my opening sentence?

81. Sometimes reading your paper aloud to yourself can help you find the places that need smoother connections between sentences and paragraphs. Read aloud slowly so you don't miss any inconsistencies. Or try reading your paper to a friend or parent. Someone with a fresh perspective may be able to point out areas for improvement.

82. Once you have found the sentences or paragraphs that need improvement, you are ready to revise your work. Revising to improve your writing is done in two steps. First, revise to improve the ideas. If you answered "No" to any of the questions on the Evaluation Checklist on page 70, go back to the paragraphs and sentences that need improvement or clarification and make the necessary changes.

83. Check to make sure your details and words give a clear picture of your subject. If they do not, add facts and sensory details. Go back to your notes and look for any facts you may have overlooked. Take out vague, nondescriptive words and replace them with more precise words.

84. Are your ideas organized in an order that will make sense to your reader? If not, reorder them to create a clear picture. Again, refer to your notes for help. Perhaps you missed some information when you wrote your first draft that would make your paper better.

85. Have you included your thoughts and feelings? If not, add them now where appropriate.

86. If you have written a paper giving instructions, are all the necessary steps included and are they in the correct order? If not, add the necessary steps and be sure to put them in the order in which they are to be performed. Have someone else read this section over to make sure the instructions are clear and complete.

87. If your paper's purpose is to make the reader change an opinion or do something to help a cause, have you included persuasive arguments and a call for action? If not, add a sentence or two that explains what your opinion is and what you hope your reader will do to support that opinion.

88. Whether your paper is creative, persuasive, informative, or expressive, it is important to cross out the sentences that do not support your main idea.

89. Proofread your paper for errors in grammar, capitalization, punctuation, and spelling. Check your sentences to make sure you've used the correct ending punctuation marks as shown in tip 42.

90. If you're not sure of the spelling of a word, look it up in your dictionary or use the Spell Check feature on your computer. Try to catch all spelling errors before you hand your paper in.

91. Check for correct usage of commas. Reading your paper aloud is also a very helpful way to discover where the pauses are. Where there is a natural pause, there is usually a comma. Here are the most common ways commas are used:

- I bought apples, bananas, grapes, cherries, and oranges.
- Boston, Massachusetts
- Yes, I'd love to come to your party.
- Mrs. Purnell, a teacher at my school, is leaving.
- July 24, 1989
- Although the moon is full, there are no werewolves out.
- The door flew open, and the wind rushed in.

If you're not sure you've placed the commas in the proper places, ask a parent or friend to read your paper. You may also refer to a grammar usage book, such as *The Elements of Style,* 3rd Edition, by William Strunk, Jr. and E.B. White (Macmillan, 1979).

92. Check your paper for proper capitalization of words. When you are checking for capitals, follow the rules on page 74:

- In a title, capitalize the first word, the last word, and all nouns, pronouns, verbs, adjectives, adverbs, and subordinating conjunctions. Articles, prepositions, and coordinating conjunctions are not capitalized.

- Begin every new sentence with a capital letter.

- Begin every direct quotation with a capital letter.

- Capitalize the first word in most lines of poetry.

- Capitalize the first words in the greeting and closing of a letter.

- Capitalize the names of particular places and things.

- Capitalize the names of days, months, and holidays, but not the seasons, such as spring.

- Capitalize names of buildings and streets.

- Capitalize names of cities, states, and countries.

- Capitalize the name of a place such as the Statue of Liberty. Do not capitalize unimportant words in the name, such as *the, of,* or *in.*

- Capitalize names of people and pets. Capitalize each word in a person's name.

- Capitalize an initial in a name and put a period after it.

- Capitalize titles when you use them with names—Doctor Coleman, President Lincoln, Madame Butterfly.

- Capitalize the pronoun I.

93. Learn to use standard proofreading marks. Here is a simple chart with the most commonly used symbols. A more complete chart may be found in your dictionary.

Proofreader's Marks

Symbol	Example	Meaning	Correction
caps	w̲	Capitalize a letter.	W
lc	8	Change the capital to a lowercase letter.	s
∧	wr∧nch	Add letters or words.	wrench
⊙	Mrs	Add a period.	Mrs.
tr	tkae	Trade places.	take
ℰ	foood	Delete something.	food
⌃	Soon	Add a comma.	Soon,
⌄⌄	Hi!	Add quotation marks.	"Hi!"
#	tooclose	Separate words.	too close
¶		Begin a new paragraph.	

94. If you have finished evaluating, improving, proofreading, and correcting your paper, you are ready to recopy your masterpiece. Now is the time to look back at your original assignment notes to find out what specific instructions were given about the format of your paper.

95. Take out a clean piece of paper. Make sure the paper is the kind your teacher has asked you to use. You don't want to copy your rough draft over and then realize the spaces between the lines are too wide!

96. Check your assignment notes and write what is required on your first page. Usually, that will be your name, the date, and your class.

97. Carefully, slowly, and as neatly as possible, start copying over your rough draft. You have put a tremendous amount of time and effort into making this paper great. Carry on that effort up to the last sentence.

98. When you are finished, add any photographs, artwork, charts, or graphs you have gathered as part of the assignment.

99. Put your paper in a protective folder so the edges and corners don't get bent, torn, or wrinkled. You've worked hard on this paper, so make it look its best!

100. Put your finished paper in your backpack *now* so you don't forget it on the day it's due.

101. Hand the paper over to your teacher. Your writing assignment is completed. Yes, you really are finished. And now you can say with pride, "I am a writer."

Congratulations!

CHAPTER 9

Lots of Lists

The Write Stuff Checklist

_____ Pencils

_____ Highlighter

._____ Pens

_____ Paper

_____ Disks (if using a computer)

_____ Dictionary

_____ Thesaurus

_____ English grammar book

_____ Note cards

Writing Assignment Checklist
✔✔✔

Assignment: _____

_____

Assignment Due Date:_____

Length of Finished Paper:

Minimum_____   Maximum_____

Prewriting Stage:

The topic of this paper is: _____

My ideas of things to write about this topic are:

_____

_____

_____

_____

I will present my ideas in this order:

_____

_____

_____

_____

Writing Stage:

First Sentence: _____

_____

Main ideas to be presented:

1. _____

_____

_____

2. _____

_____

_____

3. _____

_____

_____

Concluding sentences: _____

_____

_____

Write title: _____

Evaluating and Revising Stage (check as completed):

___Reread paper

___Correct spelling

___Correct grammar and punctuation

___Recopy for a perfect finished copy

___Turn in paper

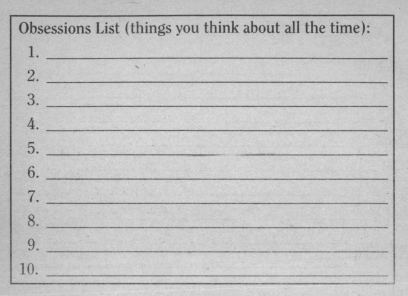

Obsessions List (things you think about all the time):

1. _____
2. _____
3. _____
4. _____
5. _____
6. _____
7. _____
8. _____
9. _____
10. _____

Tricks of the Trade

Here's a handy list of common grammar rules.

The Eight Parts of Speech

- A *noun* names a person, place, thing, action, or quality. (dancer, town, computer, George Washington)
- A *pronoun* takes the place of a noun. (I, you, he, she, it, they)
- A *verb* expresses action, happenings, or a state of being. (ran, tumble, shout, expressed, remain)
- An *adjective* modifies, or describes, a noun or a pronoun. (green, ugly, happy, careless, huge)
- An *adverb* modifies, or describes, a verb, an adjective, or another adverb. Adverbs often end in *-ly*. (greedily, hungrily, joyfully, yesterday)
- A *preposition* shows how a noun or pronoun relates to another part of a sentence. (except, around, between, into)

- A *conjunction* connects words or phrases. (across, through, against, during, because)
- An *interjection* expresses a feeling. If you are expressing a strong feeling, put an exclamation point after the interjection. (gee, Wow!, Cool!)

Other Rules

- A complete sentence must have a subject (a noun) and a predicate (a verb).
- "*i* before *e* except after *c*, or when two vowels sound like *a*, as in *neighbor* and *weigh*."
- Double the final consonant when adding a suffix to a word that begins with a vowel (except for words ending in -*er*).

      thin (root word) + -ing (suffix) – thinning

- For words that end in -*e*, drop the final -*e* when adding a suffix that begin with a vowel.

      breathe (root wood) + -ing (suffix) = breathing

- Nouns that end in -*y* often change their endings to -*i* before adding -*es*.

      guppy (root word) + -es (suffix) = guppies

Writing Topics List

When the assignment is to write about anything you want, refer to this handy topics list if you can't think of something to write about.

1. Your first visit to an amusement park

2. The most surprising thing that ever happened to you

3. Your first day at school

4. The day you got your braces or glasses

5. Lunchtime in the school cafeteria

6. How you felt when you lost your favorite Pog in a game

7. Your new pet (or your old pet)

8. The worst experience of your life

9. The best fishing experience you ever had

10. Winning (or losing) a game

11. Watching a squirrel in the backyard

12. Staying home from school because you felt sick

13. Staying home from school unexpectedly—a snow day!

14. Missing the bus

15. A friend moving away

16. Explain how to do something you do very well

17. The day the aliens came

18. Your room

19. The funniest thing that ever happened to you

20. A movie review, a review of a good television show, or a book review

21. The big storm

22. Your opinion about pollution, cafeteria food, violence on television, video games, homework, the president of the United States, or anything else

23. A visit to the beach or lake

24. A practical joke you played on someone

25. A funny thing that happened in the gym locker room

Sensory Word Bank List

Words that appeal to the five senses help to paint a clearer picture with words. Here is a word bank of sensory words to refer to when you want to add descriptive details to your paper.

Sight Words	Sound Words	Smell Words	Touch Words	Taste Words
sparkling	yelp	musty	sticky	spicy
gloomy	muffled	rotten	grainy	sour
shimmer	shriek	fragrant	furry	sweet
flushed	whimper	fresh	slimy	salty
charred	hissing	piney	smooth	bitter
glossy	screech	stale	satiny	bland
bright	laugh	pungent	sharp	lemony
sunny	chortle	lemony	pointy	tangy
cloudy	whine	fruity	gooey	tart
rainy	sneeze	stinky	clammy	briny

Misspelled Words

Some words are difficult to spell. Here is a word bank of commonly misspelled words.

accommodate	giraffe
acquaintance	guarantee
alcohol	impatient
apostrophe	jacquard
assassination	jaguar
auxiliary	jodhpur
belligerent	kaleidoscope
benign	knowledge
biscuit	languish
camouflage	laryngitis
chauffeur	lieutenant
colleague	limousine
colloquial	luxurious
conceive	maneuver
cruise	mathematics
delicious	minutia
delinquent	mischievous
deuce	moccasins
dialogue	nautilus
embarrass	neighbor
epilogue	noticeable
facetious	nuisance
feign	occasionally
foreign	orchid

parallel
parliàment
pharaoh
prologue
recommend
rendezvous
rhythm
scissors
sherbet
solemn
strengthen
surprise
suspicious
terrific
toboggan
tongue
tournament
unconscious
vacuum
veterinarian
weird
wrestle

Your Own Word Bank List

Whenever you come across a word that is unfamiliar, write it on this list. Soon you'll have lots of new words in your word bank!

_____   _____   _____

_____   _____   _____

_____   _____   _____

_____   _____   _____

_____   _____   _____

_____   _____   _____

_____   _____   _____

_____   _____   _____

_____   _____   _____

_____   _____   _____

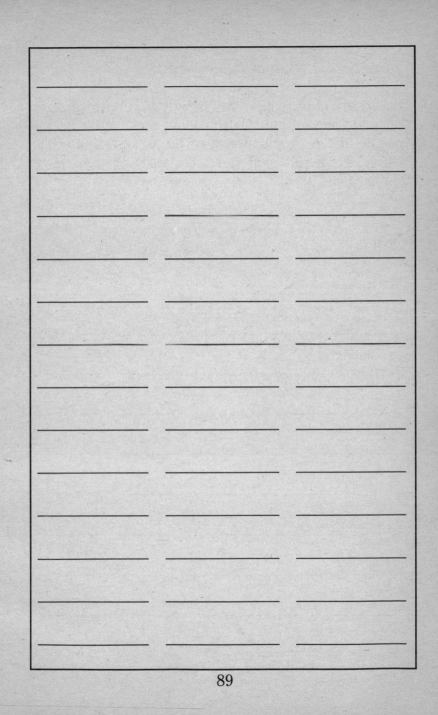

List of Papers Written

Keep track of the papers you've written. Use this list to record important information about each paper. Before you decide on a topic for your next paper, refer to this list to make sure you haven't already written on a similar topic.

Title	Date	Grade
_____	_____	_____
_____	_____	_____
_____	_____	_____
_____	_____	_____
_____	_____	_____
_____	_____	_____
_____	_____	_____
_____	_____	_____
_____	_____	_____

Title	Date	Grade
_____	_____	_____
_____	_____	_____
_____	_____	_____
_____	_____	_____
_____	_____	_____
_____	_____	_____
_____	_____	_____
_____	_____	_____
_____	_____	_____
_____	_____	_____
_____	_____	_____
_____	_____	_____
_____	_____	_____
_____	_____	_____
_____	_____	_____

Bibliography

Bell, Kathleen L., Francess Freeman Paden, and Susan Duffy Schaffrath. *McDougal, Littell English*. Evanston, IL: McDougal, Littell & Company, 1987.

Charlton, James. *The Writer's Quotation Book*. New York, NY: James Charlton Associates, 1985.

Fitzhenry, Robert I., ed. *Fitzhenry & Whiteside Book of Quotations*. Ontario: Fitzhenry & Whiteside, 1986.

Goldberg, Natalie. *Writing Down the Bones*. Boston, MA: Shambhala Publications, 1986.

Kinneavy, James L. and John E. Warriner. *Elements of Writing*. Orlando, FL: Holt, Rinehart and Winston, 1993.

Provost, Gary. *100 Ways to Improve Your Writing*. New York, NY: Penguin Group, 1985.

Strunk, Jr., William and E. B. White. *The Elements of Style (3rd Edition)*. New York, NY: Macmillan, 1979.

INDEX

Notes

Notes